Managing
Up

Pocket Mentor Series

The *Pocket Mentor* Series offers immediate solutions to common challenges managers face on the job every day. Each book in the series is packed with handy tools, self-tests, and real-life examples to help you identify your strengths and weaknesses and hone critical skills. Whether you're at your desk, in a meeting, or on the road, these portable guides enable you to tackle the daily demands of your work with greater speed, savvy, and effectiveness.

Books in the series:

Leading Teams

Running Meetings

Managing Time

Managing Projects

Coaching People

Giving Feedback

Leading People

Negotiating Outcomes

Writing for Business

Giving Presentations

Understanding Finance

Dismissing an Employee

Creating a Business Plan

Managing Stress

Delegating Work

Shaping Your Career

Persuading People

Managing Crises

Managing Up

Managing Up

Up

Expert Solutions to Everyday Challenges

Harvard Business Press

Boston, Massachusetts

Library of Congress Cataloging-in-Publication Data
Managing up : expert solutions to everyday challenges.
     p. cm. — (Pocket mentor series)
   Includes bibliographical references.
   ISBN 978-1-4221-2277-8
   1. Managing your boss.
   HF5548.83.M363 2008
   650.1'3—dc22

                         2008003082

The paper used in this publication meets the requirements of the American National
Standard for Permanence of Paper for Publications and Documents in Libraries and
Archives Z39.48-1992.

Contents

Mentors' Message: Why Manage Up?   ix

Managing Up: The Basics   1

What Is Managing Up?   3

Helpful information on the advantages of managing up.

The benefits of managing up   4

The dangers of *not* managing up   6

Developing a Relationship with Your Manager   9

Strategies for forging a strong partnership with your boss.

Acknowledging the power differential   10

How you can drive the relationship-building process   11

Understanding your manager   13

Understanding yourself   14

Managing expectations   16

Promoting your manager's goals   19

Communicating with Your Manager   25

Ideas for effectively communicating with your boss and handling disagreements.

Understanding your manager's communication style   26

Using communication to boost productivity   28

Using listening and questioning   32

Disagreeing with your manager   33

Negotiating with Your Manager   39

Tactics for designing win–win solutions with your boss.

Demonstrating your credibility   40

Identifying priorities   44

Negotiating strategically   46

Tips and Tools   49

Tools for Managing Up   51

Worksheets to help you understand your manager, understand yourself, monitor the effectiveness of your relationship with your boss, and negotiate effectively with your manager.

Test Yourself   57

A helpful review of concepts presented in this guide. Take it before and after you've read the guide, to see how much you've learned.

Answers to test questions   61

To Learn More 65

Further titles of articles and books if you want to go more deeply into the topic.

Sources for Managing Up 73

Notes 75

For you to use as ideas come to mind.

Mentors' Message: Why Manage Up?

You're talking with a friend, and you ask her how her new job is going. She says, "Ever since I started managing up, things have gotten a lot better." You cringe. To your ear, "managing up" sounds distasteful—and smacks of political maneuvering.

But managing up is not political game playing. Rather, it's a conscious approach to working with your supervisor toward goals that are important to both of you—an approach that can enable you to exert your own influence on those goals. Through managing up, you build a productive working relationship with your boss and, together, use your complementary strengths to deliver value to your company.

To manage up, you need to master a specific set of skills, including knowing how to build a positive, productive working relationship with your boss, how to communicate effectively with him or her (including disagreeing with your manager's ideas and suggestions), and how to negotiate work priorities with your supervisor.

This guide provides useful recommendations, strategies, and hands-on tools for strengthening these skills—so you, your boss, and your organization can gain all the benefits of managing up.

Katie Carlone and Linda A. Hill, Mentors

Katie Carlone is a consultant with twenty years of experience in providing tools and workshops to enable sales and marketing professionals to achieve performance goals. She specializes in analyzing training needs and developing solutions that are effective and practical, such as a knowledge management tool that provides just-in-time learning and speeds new products to market.

From her more than twenty years of extensive field work, Linda A. Hill has helped managers create the conditions for effective management in today's flatter and increasingly diverse organizations. She is a professor and chair of the Leadership Initiative at Harvard Business School. She is also the author of the best-selling *Becoming a Manager* (Harvard Business School Press), and the content expert for *Coaching for Results* and *Managing Direct Reports*, award-winning interactive programs from Harvard Business School Publishing.

Managing Up: The Basics

What Is
Managing Up?

MANAGING UP IS A conscious approach to working with your manager toward mutually agreed-upon goals that are in the best interests of you, your boss, and your organization. It is not mere political maneuvering; rather, it is a process of influencing your manager to make decisions that benefit both of you as well as the company.

The benefits of managing up

Managing up: To many people, this phrase smacks of manipulation, corporate "cozying up," or out-and-out apple polishing performed by those seeking merely to advance in their careers. But managing up is none of these things. And it's vital for good reasons. Those who master the art of managing up get the resources they need to do the best job, not only for themselves but also for their bosses and companies. They also actively pursue a healthy and productive working relationship with their boss based on mutual respect and understanding. They know their own and their manager's strengths, weaknesses, goals, work styles, and needs.

People who manage up also understand that they and their bosses are mutually dependent on one another. What does this mutual dependence look like? Your boss needs cooperation, reliability, and honesty from you. And you need your boss to forge links to the rest of your organization, to set priorities, and to obtain critical resources (whether personnel, funding, office space, equipment, or other resources essential to carrying out your responsibilities).

When handled skillfully, managing up facilitates the entire management process by making use of all available expertise and resources to develop solutions to problems rather than just talking about them, ignoring them, or covering them up. A strong relationship with your manager can increase your effectiveness and make your work life easier. It also helps you:

- Foster open communication, so your manager will be more open to your opinions and ideas.

- Support the organization. Working as partners, you and your manager can make significant contributions to achieving results beyond your work group.

Consider this example of the benefits of managing up. Sam, a new director with a formal work style, replaced someone who had a looser and more intuitive style. Sam preferred written reports and structured meetings. Carla, one of his direct reports, knew the importance of managing up. She observed Sam's work style, identifying the kinds and frequency of information he wanted. She sent ahead background reports and discussion agendas before meeting with Sam. The result was highly productive meetings and innovative problem solving that improved the entire team's performance.

"The meeting of two personalities is like the contact of two chemical substances; if there is any reaction, both are transformed."
—Carl Jung

The dangers of *not* managing up

Without a strong relationship with your manager, misunderstandings and lack of communication can divert time and attention from your group's efforts to serve customers and meet business objectives. If you neglect this relationship, your goals and priorities may be at odds with those of your manager, leading to frustration and discontent for one or both parties. Communication between you and your manager may be ineffective at best, or even avoided whenever possible. And your performance appraisal rating may suffer, reducing your chances for pay increases, promotions, and career expansion. Your supervisor may be forced to work around you and begin to direct the people who report to you.

A weak relationship between you and your manager can have negative consequences for the broader organization as well. Without a commitment to shared goals and objectives by you and your manager, bottom-line results for your department or team and the organization as a whole may suffer. Communication breakdowns can lead to misunderstandings and poor morale, resulting in less-than-effective performance in your team. And low morale, in turn, can hurt customer relationships.

Here's one example of what can happen when a person fails to manage up. Remember Carla, who worked hard to understand

and adapt to Sam's work style? Larry, another manager in Sam's group, didn't bother to do so. He found Sam's style too controlling. He seldom sent background information to Sam before a meeting or problem-solving session, and was often blindsided by unanticipated questions from Sam when they did meet. Sam found their meetings inefficient and frustrating, and eventually asked for Larry's resignation.

Many people find it helpful to think of managing up as a constant process, "like being in a good marriage," writes business author Deborah Singer Dobson in her book *Managing Up*. "You don't go around saying you've done enough modifying your behavior for your spouse," Dobson points out. "We're all in the business of modifying our behavior on a daily basis in relationships that are important to us." However, once you and your boss have built a trusting, mutually beneficial relationship, the time required to nurture and cultivate that relationship should lessen, because you've constructed a solid foundation.

Given the importance of managing up, what's the best way to start crafting this mutually beneficial relationship with your manager? The following sections cover three crucial practices: developing a positive, productive relationship with your boss, communicating effectively with your manager and handling disagreements strategically, and negotiating strategically with your manager. We'll start by focusing on how to cultivate a good relationship with your boss. But first, complete the self-assessment "How well do you manage up?" to test your current capacity for managing up.

How well do you manage up?

For each statement below, check yes or no to indicate whether the statement applies to you.

	Yes	No
1. I am aware of my manager's expectations of me and have articulated my expectations of my boss.		
2. When I negotiate with my boss, I use *we* and *I* language.		
3. I regularly inform my manager of what I'm working on.		
4. I notify my manager of problems promptly and suggest several solutions to consider.		
5. My boss and I deal with disagreements as they arise.		
6. My relationship with my manager is characterized by trust and reliability.		
7. I understand my boss's pressures and priorities.		
8. My manager never steps in to direct one or more of my employees.		
9. I've asked my manager openly about his or her management style and likes and dislikes and have adapted my style to my boss's as much as possible.		
10. I take as much time as necessary to communicate with my manager about important matters.		
11. I seek ways to exert my influence on other department leaders, customers, and suppliers so as to support my manager's goals.		
Total		

Interpreting your score:

- If you answered yes to most or all of the statements, you have significant managing-up capability. But read on to see what else you can learn about this important business skill. For any statements to which you answered no, keep these in mind as you read this book.

- If you answered no to most or all of the statements, you would benefit from learning more about how to manage up effectively. The remaining chapters in this book provide helpful suggestions and strategies.

Developing a Relationship with Your Manager

I T IS TO YOUR benefit to assume the primary responsibility for shaping your relationship with your manager. Such a proactive approach goes a long way toward establishing a foundation of trust and rapport, and toward creating a relationship that matches your styles and needs. From the start, let your manager know the value you place on your relationship. Don't wait for a crisis to prompt you into action.

Acknowledging the power differential

Relationships of all kinds in your professional life are crucial to your business success—whether these relationships are with key customers, suppliers, or vendors. Your relationship with your boss is simply another critical relationship.

However, the boss–subordinate relationship is a special case, because it has a power differential. As business writer Liz Simpson explains, "To put it bluntly, your boss can fire you but you can't fire him. This power differential will always affect the dynamics of your interactions with your manager."

Management experts John Gabarro and John Kotter have written that the power differential between a subordinate and boss can result in some frustration when your actions are constrained by your boss's decisions. "The way in which a manager handles these frustrations," Gabarro and Kotter have explained, "largely depends on his or her predisposition toward dependence on authority figures."

These experts recommend understanding and avoiding two common responses to the realities of the power differential between a manager and his or her boss:

- **Counterdependency.** Counterdependent managers unconsciously resent their boss's authority. Viewing the boss almost as an institutional enemy, they may start arguments (especially with authoritarian bosses) just for the sake of fighting.

- **Dependency.** Dependent managers, Gabarro and Kotter maintain, "swallow their anger and behave in a very compliant fashion when the boss makes what they know to be a poor decision."

If you have either of these attitudes toward authority, you may find it difficult to change. However, by being aware of these two extremes as well as the range between them, you can more easily see where your own tendencies fall and how these tendencies might be negatively affecting your relationship with your boss.

How you can drive the relationship-building process

The following guidelines can help you build a productive working relationship with your manager:

- Think about the relationship as a partnership, and recognize your shared objectives.

What Would YOU Do?

Getting Josef's Number

J ENNA WAS RECENTLY hired as a division manager at Nimbus Corporation, a global market research agency located in Germany. Jenna comes from Sweden, so she's just getting to know her new supervisor, Josef, the division vice president. After several weeks on the job, Jenna figured out a few things about Josef. For example, he tends to want written reports on issues before talking with her about the details. Also, he gets irritable when she asks him questions first thing Monday morning.

Jenna knows she can't communicate or collaborate effectively with him unless she understands more about him. However, she's not sure what additional things she needs to know.

What would YOU do? The mentors will suggest a solution in *What You COULD Do.*

- Come to an agreement about mutual expectations, key responsibilities, standards of performance, and measures of success.

- Ask your manager to share her own goals and objectives with you. You can then assist her in meeting her own performance commitments to the organization.

- Let your manager know what you can do for her.

- Provide information to your manager in accordance with her preferred style.

- Deliver the results your manager requires and needs. And exceed those requirements and needs whenever possible.

- Be honest and dependable.

- Be open and receptive to feedback and advice, rather than becoming defensive.

- Anticipate, forewarn, and share potential problems with your manager on a timely basis, before a crisis develops. Work together to create solutions that head off problems before they emerge.

- Use your manager's time wisely. Do not take up a manager's time and resources with trivial matters.

Tip: Make your manager a partner. Don't put him or her in the role of adversary.

Understanding your manager

To develop your relationship with your manager, you need to be able to see the world through her eyes. Try to identify the pressures she faces. It is critical for you to understand her perspectives and look for common ground with your own. Also, learn as much as you can about your manager's strengths, weaknesses, organizational and personal objectives, personal interests, and preferred working style. Be aware of her blind spots and trigger points, so you can respond appropriately if and when they arise.

Tip: Practice seeing the world through your managers' eyes and positioning ideas from his or her perspective.

You can learn about your manager in a variety of ways. For example, ask her openly about her management style, her likes and dislikes, and any unique needs she has. Speak with other staff members about their insights into your manager, and ask for their advice and feedback. Finally, closely observe your manager as she pursues objectives and interacts with others. What do her behavior and approach to her job suggest about how best to work with her?

The table "Accommodating your boss's work style" shows questions that you can ask yourself to determine how best to adjust to your boss's preferences.

Understanding yourself

In addition to understanding your manager, you need to develop a clear understanding of yourself and how you work. That's because you are an important half of this relationship.

Accommodating your boss's work style

Use this chart to determine your manager's work style and develop strategies for accommadating it.

Questions to ask	Actions to take
Does she prefer a more formal and organized approach?	Make sure that meetings with her have set agendas.
Does he become impatient or inattentive if you veer off the topic at hand?	Keep digressions, background detail, and informal chitchat to a minimum.
How does she process information best?	If she likes to be able to study it by herself, give it to her in written form. If she likes to be able to ask questions, present it to her in person.
What is his decision-making style?	If he's a high-involvement manager, touch base with him often on an ad hoc basis. If he prefers to delegate, keep him abreast of important changes and major problems, but handle the other details on your own.
How does she handle conflict?	If she seems to thrive on it, be prepared for lively, spontaneous exchanges with her. If these exchanges become heated, she isn't necessarily angry with you. If she tends to minimize conflict, respect that preference without falling into the trap of telling her only the happy news. She needs to know about failures and important problems, but it may be best to inform her about these in private.

Source: Liz Simpson, "Why Managing Up Matters," *Harvard Management Update*, August 2002, 4.

Ask yourself the same questions you asked about your manager. Specifically, what is your personal work style? What are your strengths, weaknesses, blind spots, and trigger points? Once you understand how you and your manager work, you can learn how to maximize each other's strengths and minimize each other's weaknesses.

Keep in mind that you have more control over your own actions and reactions than you do over your manager's. Using what you know about your manager, modify your own approach as best you can to arrive at a style of interaction that works for both of you.

Managing expectations

Setting clear expectations is an important step in building a productive working relationship with your boss. Ask your manager to describe her expectations of you. If your manager cannot articulate her expectations, send an informal written memo outlining your understanding of those expectations, and ask for feedback and agreement. Then, clarify any outstanding issues in a follow-up conversation.

If your manager responds better to a meeting than a written interchange, set up a series of informal conversations to discuss mutual roles, responsibilities, and measures of success. Try to ask for feedback on a periodic basis, so you can determine whether your boss's expectations have changed.

Though each manager will have different expectations depending on his or her department's and company's strategic plans, most managers expect specific behaviors of their direct reports. The following are examples of these behaviors:

- **Offer ideas.** Don't be shy about offering your creative ideas to your boss. She wants to hear them, because even seemingly far-fetched or crazy ideas can spark spectacular, unexpected successes in a team's efforts.

- **Get involved in your own team's difficulties.** Step in the moment one of your own direct reports falls behind with his or her commitments, when an interpersonal conflict crops up, or when a crisis erupts. And deliver bad news to your boss yourself.

- **Collaborate with peers.** Overcome differences between you and peer managers throughout your organization, so you work together effectively—even if you dislike one another.

- **Lead initiatives.** Don't be reluctant to associate yourself with unproven ideas, especially those that cross functional or unit boundaries. Raise your hand for cross-organizational initiatives and projects.

- **Develop your own subordinates.** Take as much interest in your employees' development as you do in your own—if not more. Go out of your way to provide constructive criticism and praise with your people when they need it. And invest time and careful attention in performance reviews, supplying your people with specific, candid, and useful feedback.

- **Stay current.** Regularly read and watch the news. What happens in the world affects what happens with your team, your company's marketplace, and the firm's competition. Also, know what's going on with your company's customers—how they're changing, and how technology and world events are affecting their plans.

- **Drive your own growth.** Seek perpetual education and development. You don't necessarily have to go to night classes or begin a new degree program. Instead, find exposure to new people and ideas. Seek feedback from your boss, and accept demanding assignments. All of these experiences will further your development as a manager.

- **Be a player for all seasons.** Demonstrate positive behaviors and attitudes even during hard times. You'll sustain your ability to motivate and inspire your own people no matter what's going on around you.

Tip: Openly acknowledge the value of your manager's input and leadership when you successfully address a problem or seize an opportunity.

It is also important for you to let your manager know what *you* expect of her. Clarify your expectations during a face-to-face meeting, and ask for agreement. For example, you might say something like, "For me to be effective on this project, I need clear direction from you on what our unit's strategic priorities are and what resources we have available to support those priorities." The key is to communicate your expectations to find out whether they are realistic. You may need to persuade your boss to accept the most important ones.

If your expectations don't match your manager's, try to negotiate an agreement that works for both of you. Periodically reassess this agreement, and modify it as you need to.

EXPECTATIONS *n* 1: prospects, especially of success or gain

Promoting your manager's goals

Just as you hope and expect that your manager will support your goals, you should do what you can to support your manager's goals. You can use your influence and relationships within the organization to make your manager and your entire team look good.

For example, increase your sphere of influence in areas that can affect your manager's goals—such as other departments, customers, and suppliers. To illustrate, if you have a positive working relationship with the heads of other departments, you can more readily become aware of ways in which other departments can help yours—by providing needed information, needed personnel, and other important resources.

But in increasing your sphere of influence with other department leaders, customers, and suppliers, engage people from where they are, not where you would like them to be. That is, before trying to influence anyone, make a point of understanding his or her mind-set. For instance, if you want to persuade the head of another department to support an initiative that your boss is advocating, first determine how backing the initiative would help your colleague solve problems important in his own department.

Tip: Make your manager—and your organization—look good by achieving or exceeding goals and objectives.

Also, when enhancing your sphere of influence, know that you'll be seeking to influence the actions of others over whom you lack authority. In these situations, offering advice, providing feedback, and sharing your reactions and perspectives can constitute worthwhile "investments" in your relationships with these other individuals.

Finally, recognize that to exert your influence and promote your manager's goals most effectively, you may have to relinquish some control and empower others, particularly with your own employees. For instance, by delegating to your direct reports instead of micromanaging them, you enable them to master new skills that could be important to your team's or department's (and thus your boss's) priorities.

Steps for Developing a Relationship with Your Manager

1. **Understand your manager's and your own styles and perspectives.**

   Seek to understand your manager's leadership style, likes and dislikes, and any unique needs. Then, clarify the same things about yourself. Using what you know about your manager, modify your own approach as best you can to arrive at a style of interaction that works for both of you.

2. **Determine how you will work together.**

   Take the lead in proposing ground rules for your working relationship—for example, mode and frequency of communication, the limits of your decision-making authority (which decisions can you make on your own, and which do you need to run by your manager?), how you will let each other know about potential problems and how you will approach them, and mechanisms and timing for exchanging feedback.

3. **Agree on goals and expectations.**

   Set up a series of informal conversations to discuss roles, responsibilities, and measures of success. If your manager prefers to communicate in writing, send an informal written memo that outlines your understanding of his expectations and your expectations of him, and ask for feedback. Then, clarify any outstanding issues in a follow-up conversation. Be as specific as you can in defining deadlines and deliverables.

4. **Revisit your goals and interaction process, and revise as needed.**
   Meet with your manager periodically to review goals and expectations and to determine whether they have changed or need to be changed. Similarly, you should discuss your relationship explicitly and exchange feedback on what works and what doesn't work. Use what you learn to refine your interaction process, and check back within a defined period of time to see whether your refinements have been effective.

What You COULD Do.

Remember Jenna's concern about how to better understand her new boss, Josef?

Here's what the mentors suggest:

In addition to understanding whether Josef is a listener or a reader and when he likes to receive information, Jenna should also learn as much as she can about what Josef's goals and daily pressures consist of. By knowing what Josef hopes to achieve professionally and what kinds of challenges he has to deal with in his role, Jenna can help support Josef's objectives with her own efforts in her group. For example, if one of Josef's goals is to trim costs in the division, Jenna could support that objective by identifying ways to streamline redundancies in her group's processes or systems. Supporting your supervisor's goals is a major component of managing up.

Communicating
with Your Manager

A POSITIVE WORKING RELATIONSHIP with your boss hinges on effective communication, whether face-to-face or in written form. The sections below provide guidelines for understanding your manager's communication style, using communication to boost productivity, using listening and questioning effectively, and disagreeing with your manager in ways that lead to mutually attractive solutions.

Understanding your manager's communication style

We all have our own preferences for communication—including how we want to receive information, solve problems, and make decisions. Communicating with your boss in a way that matches her preferred style can go a long way toward building a positive, productive relationship.

It all starts with understanding your manager's communication style. First, determine whether she is a listener or a reader. Then present information to her accordingly. Listeners want to hear information first and read about it later. Readers like to see written reports first and then talk with you about them.

Also determine whether your manager prefers detailed facts and figures or just an overview. Finally, determine the frequency of your manager's need for information. Is she someone who prefers day-to-day, hands-on involvement in your projects or someone who would rather delegate and receive updates and progress checks as needed? Tailor your communications accordingly.

Some managers find it difficult to know how much information to provide their bosses. The quantity of information a supervisor needs about what her direct report is doing will vary depending on that boss's style, situation, and confidence in the employee. But many bosses need more information than their subordinates supply on their own. And many subordinates think their bosses know more than he or she really does. To be effective, recognize that you may underestimate what your boss needs to know. Find ways to keep her informed through processes that fit her style.

You may also wonder what kind of information to provide your boss; namely, should you deliver only good news? Only bad news? Both kinds? This can be challenging if you have the sense that your supervisor doesn't like to hear about problems. The fact is, many bosses inadvertently send signals that they want to hear only happy news. But for the sake of the team and the entire company, every boss must know about failures as well as successes. If you've got a good-news-only boss, find ways to get important information to her promptly.

One last point about understanding your boss's communication style: a supervisor's communication preferences not only reflect her work style; they can also reflect her deeply held values. And if you don't take time to grasp and demonstrate respect for those preferences, your relationship with your boss may stumble. Consider this example, related by business writer Liz Simpson in her article "Why Managing Up Matters" (*Harvard Management Update*, August 2002):

> One CFO . . . drove his boss crazy by always closing the office door when they were discussing things. The boss prided himself on his open-door policy and felt that his CFO's action compromised his integrity. [According to the CFO's coach], "While he was extremely competent in other ways, he never got himself out of that habit [of closing the door], and when there was a restructuring he was one of those released."
>
> The boss's preference for an open door was more than a pet peeve; it was a symbol of his availability to his employees. By failing to notice that preference, [the CFO] was inadvertently sending the message that he didn't support one of his boss's strongly held values.

COMMUNICATION *n* 1: the exchange of thoughts, messages, or information, as by speech, signals, writing, or behavior

---

Using communication to boost productivity

Adapting your communication style to your boss's can help the two of you work together more smoothly. But you can also use communication between you and your manager to boost productivity in your department. To that end, keep in mind that you are responsible for creating the conditions for your own success. Let your manager know in what areas you will need help or organizational resources. Be honest with your boss about what you can and cannot handle. And be sure to explain to your manager just how you see a particular project being accomplished and where you may need additional help to meet that goal.

> **Tip:** Keep your manager informed. Provide a "heads up" so that he or she knows about a possible impending crisis before it happens.

When discussing deadlines, use specific language. Do not leave room for assumptions. It is too easy to fall into the trap of agreeing with your manager to meet a deadline of "sometime next week," "ASAP," or "as soon as you can get to it." These sorts of agreements most often lead to decreased productivity and major misunderstandings.

In addition, don't be shy about communicating your interest in working on other projects or your desire to improve your skills in a specific area. Help your manager see how such an assignment could have long-term benefits for both of you and for the organization—for example, by enabling you to acquire new skills important to your department's or company's competitive strategy.

Also, identify your goals and objectives for each exchange of information with your manager, to let her know what is important to you. Real productivity results only when both of you are working toward mutually agreed-upon goals and objectives.

Communicate the results of solutions or approaches to your manager, so he or she can share them with others in the organization.

Finally, ask for clarification of any requests or pieces of information from your manager that are unclear to you. If you don't ask questions, you may misunderstand what you're hearing from your manager and take a project down the wrong path.

Steps for Presenting Problems or Opportunities to Your Manager

1. **Describe the problem or opportunity to your boss.**
   Provide a general overview of the problem, and show the specific impact that the problem is having on your work and on the organization's goals. If you have identified an opportunity, show the potential benefits if the opportunity is pursued. Explain that if the two of you solve this problem or seize this opportunity, work can proceed more smoothly toward mutually agreed-upon objectives, and the organization will benefit significantly.

2. **Identify your solution or approach.**
   Explain how you have already tried to solve the problem and what you have learned from those attempts. Recommend a specific solution or approach, along with alternatives to provide your manager with options. Most managers prefer to hear about your solutions

or approaches, not your problems or ideas. Without your reasonable solution or creative approach, your manager may hear your problem or opportunity as simply another complaint or wild idea.

Also, clearly define each possible alternative, along with pros and cons and potential risks or barriers. Explain the logic that led you to your recommended solution or approach. You want your manager to be aware that you carefully considered all possible outcomes before drawing a conclusion.

3. **Explain the implications of the solution or approach.**
Consider the impact that your solution or approach will have on yourself and others, including your manager and the organization as a whole. Avoid focusing on everyone else involved and forgetting about yourself or, conversely, focusing on yourself and forgetting about everyone else. Be sure to make explicit that the problem and solution, or opportunity and approach, can have far-reaching effects on the goals of the organization.

4. **Discuss the benefits of your solution or approach.**
Focus your discussion on the benefits to be gained from implementation of your solution to the problem or approach to the opportunity. The specific features of the solution, or how it will be implemented, are less important at this stage. Give concrete examples of the kinds of benefits your proposed solution or approach could provide to your manager and to the organization. If you have tested your solution or approach on a small scale with good results, say so. This can be a strong point in gaining commitment for your solution.

5. **Accept responsibility for the outcome.**
Let your manager know that you are willing to take the responsibility for the outcome of your solution or approach. This is an important

part of your discussion and demonstrates your commitment to ensuring success. Also actively engage your manager in developing a final action plan for addressing the problem you've identified or taking advantage of the opportunity you've presented.

Using listening and questioning

As the previous section suggests, your skill as a listener and questioner drives your ability to get the most out of regular interactions with your manager. Concentrate on being an effective listener as you engage with your boss during everyday business activities. As you listen, try to identify the messages behind your manager's words and behaviors. For example, if your boss seems under stress, seek to determine what's causing the stress and how you can help.

During every conversation or meeting with your manager, also let your boss know about any questions that you have and any areas requiring further clarification before the encounter is over.

Remember to listen actively to help put yourself in your manager's shoes. Offer verbal feedback ("I see" or "I know what you mean") and nonverbal feedback (nodding or smiling to indicate your understanding) to your manager. And withhold judgment to show your interest and empathy.

LISTENING *n* 1: paying attention to hear something properly

Also keep in mind that most people have a tendency to provide their superiors with too little information, not too much, and that they often provide it too late. Ask questions to determine how much information your boss wants from you and how frequently and promptly she would like you to provide it.

You can also use questions to promote a more collaborative relationship with your manager. By asking questions, you can:

- Gather new information about your boss.

- Stimulate conversation and show your interest and receptivity to your manager's business objectives.

- Develop a better understanding of your manager's viewpoints.

- Check for agreement on critical points.

- Continue to build trust and rapport.

- Verify or clarify information.

Disagreeing with your manager

Many people hesitate to disagree with their managers. They worry that they will be viewed as negative by their boss or that they will trigger a defensive reaction. But most managers highly value alternative perspectives—and most report that they do not hear as many of them as they would like. By bringing new information or views to light, you can help your manager make more informed decisions. The key is to disagree in a constructive manner. The following practices can help:

- **Tie your ideas or feedback into your organization's and your manager's goals.** For example, "I think this other customer database would help us cut costs more than the one you're thinking about, and decreasing costs seems to be on everyone's agenda these days."

- **Provide your manager with actionable suggestions rather than simply raising objections.** For instance, "What if we talked with some other companies that have used this database, to see what their experience has been like and whether they have any specific concerns about the software."

- **Explain how your ideas could help avoid potential pitfalls or overcome risks.** To illustrate, "The database I'm advocating may give us a better chance of preventing security breaches, and it can be installed as a stand-alone program rather than having to be integrated with our other IT systems."

- **Give your manager some alternative choices.** For example, "In addition to considering replacing our current database, we can also think about upgrading it or outsourcing the database functionality entirely."

- **Reflect her concerns in your conversation.** For instance, "I understand that you're worried about how quickly and affordably we can train the staff on the new database. I've been doing some research into this, and I've found a local consultant whose fees are pretty reasonable and whose track record with other client companies like ours is impressive."

In all your communication with your manager, remember that if you and she share the same goals, disagreements between you will likely not happen often.

The table "Take the 'managing up' challenge" lets you evaluate how well an employee has communicated with her boss.

Take the "managing up" challenge

Now that you've learned more about how to communicate effectively with your manager, try your hand at evaluating how well Grace, a regional manager for a business-to-business software company, has communicated with her boss, Randy. Read the transcription of their meeting below; then follow the instructions for evaluating Grace's effectiveness.

Transcription:

Grace: Randy, do you have a minute? I'd like to discuss some of these objectives you've given us.

Randy: Sure, have a seat.

Grace: I hope I'm not interrupting. I know how busy you are these days.

Randy: Not at all. You know I like to discuss these kinds of issues in person. E-mail leads to too many misunderstandings.

Grace: Okay—thanks. One of our objectives here is to "increase efficiency of our internal processes." That's pretty broad. Where, specifically, do think our internal processes are falling short?

Randy: Actually, one of the higher-ups put that language in there. I agree that it's vague, and I've asked them to send some clarification.

Grace: Great. You've also said we should try to increase sales to service-industry customers by 15%. Most of our salespeople aren't used to dealing with the service industry. So I think a bit of training might be necessary to reach this goal. What do you think?

Randy: I'd agree with that.

Grace : I'll try to handle the specifics of how we'll do that training and get you a proposal sometime in the next few weeks.

Randy: Sounds good.

Grace: Would you like something brief, with a rough estimate of costs, or something more in-depth, with a detailed cost breakdown?

Randy: There's no need for the body of the proposal to be more than a page or two, but I'd like a detailed cost breakdown. It's getting harder and harder to get approval for training funds these days.

continued

Grace: All right. Finally, this last objective. It says we should start pushing the updates to accounting software to all of our current clients. With all due respect, I think that might be a mistake.

Randy: Really? Why's that?

Grace: It was only last year that we released the most recent version of the software. A lot of our clients are small businesses, and I think they'll resent the fact that we're already pushing them to invest in a new version of the software. You've said yourself that our small-business customers are the backbone of our sales strategy, and I think they're the ones most likely to be alienated by this push.

Randy: You make a good point. Perhaps we should revise the objective to make it clear that, for now, we should only be suggesting the update to our larger customers who like to stay on the cutting edge of this technology.

Grace: Thanks, Randy.

Instructions:

Place a checkmark next to each statement that you think represents something Grace did effectively during this conversation with her manager.

- ☐ 1. Grace communicated in the style that her manager prefers.
- ☐ 2. She used specific language when discussing deadlines.
- ☐ 3. She asked for clarification on parts of the plan that were unclear.
- ☐ 4. She sought information on her manager's preferences.
- ☐ 5. She checked for agreement on critical points.
- ☐ 6. When disagreeing, she tied her feedback into her organization's and her manager's goals.
- ☐ 7. When disagreeing, she provided her manager with several alternative choices.

Interpreting your responses:

The correct statements to check are 1, 3, 4, 5, and 6. Explanations are provided below.

1. **Check:** Grace dropped in for a face-to-face chat, which she knew was Randy's preferred style of communication.

2. **Don't check:** Grace said she would get a proposal to Randy "sometime in the next few weeks." This is vague, and Randy might interpret it differently from what Grace intended.

3. **Check:** Grace asked Randy to clarify the vague objective about improving internal processes.

4. **Check:** Grace asked Randy how he would prefer her to structure her proposal.

5. **Check:** Grace made sure that Randy agreed with her that the sales team would need additional training.

6. **Check:** When Grace disagreed with Randy's idea about pushing the new accounting software update to clients, she framed her disagreement in terms of the company's desire to prioritize relationships with its small-business customers. She also noted that Randy himself considered these customers a priority.

7. **Don't check:** When Grace disagreed about pushing the new accounting software version on customers, she did not come up with an alternative. Instead, Randy suggested one. If Grace had offered some alternatives, she would have helped to make Randy's job easier, which would have further strengthened their relationship.

Negotiating with Your Manager

T HERE ARE OFTEN times when you need to persuade your manager to view a situation from your perspective and to take action as a result. In these situations, you'll need to call on your negotiating skills to arrive at a mutually agreeable solution with your boss. The sections below introduce an issue that managers and their direct reports frequently must negotiate—work priorities—and provide guidelines for demonstrating your credibility with your boss (a crucial ingredient whenever you're trying to negotiate and persuade) and negotiating strategically with your boss.

Tip: In negotiating with your manager, be direct. Ask for what you want and need, rather than assuming that your manager will automatically know these things.

Demonstrating your credibility

As in any situation where you're seeking to persuade another person of the merits of your case, demonstrating your credibility can help you negotiate effectively with your manager. Credibility is the cornerstone of persuasion and negotiation. Without it, your boss may not commit time or resources to your idea or proposal. Your credibility manifests itself on two levels:

- **Your ideas.** Are your ideas sound? For example, does your notion to focus your efforts on developing a new product offering make sense in light of current market conditions and business concerns? Have you thought through all the ramifications?

- **You as a person.** Are you believable? Trustworthy? Sincere? Have you proved yourself knowledgeable and well informed? For instance, if you've proposed a new offering, do you have a solid understanding of its specifications, target markets, customers, and competition? Can your boss perceive that understanding?

Credibility can be understood in terms of this simple but powerful formula:

$$Credibility = Trust + Expertise$$

The more trust you earn and expertise you accumulate, the more credible you *and* your ideas will become to your boss. Let's take a closer look at the two elements of the credibility equation, starting with trust. The following actions can help you accumulate trust with your boss:

- **Be sincere.** Demonstrate your conviction that your idea is worth your boss's time and attention. When your supervisor sees you as sincere and committed, she will more likely trust you.

?What Would YOU Do?

Is It Really "My Way or the Highway"?

D AVID REVIEWED THE schedule for a new project that his boss, Maria, had asked him to take on. The project involved preparing a series of reports for another department in the company. After reviewing the schedule, he concluded that the deadline was impossible to meet. He couldn't understand why Maria had agreed to the schedule while discussing it with the other department. He also couldn't understand why she hadn't sought his input before signing off on it.

David thought about going ahead with the project and trying to meet the deadline, but he knew his team would fail—and then everyone would look bad. He was tempted to write a memo to Maria protesting the schedule before beginning the project. But he worried that that would antagonize her, and he needed her support. Surely, thought David, there must be a way to disagree with your boss without jeopardizing the project, the team, or your job.

What would YOU do? The mentors will suggest a solution in *What You COULD Do.*

- **Build a track record of trustworthiness.** Follow through on promises and commitments you've made to your boss. By *behaving* in a trustworthy manner, you earn a reputation for *being* trustworthy.

- **Encourage the exploration of ideas.** Listen to your boss's concerns to encourage dialogue and demonstrate your openness to her perspectives.

- **Put your boss's best interests first.** When your supervisor believes that you have her interests in mind, she will tend to trust you and your ideas more.

- **Use candor.** When you own up to your flaws, your boss will see you as a truthful person—on the assumption that most individuals try to conceal their faults. Thus, an honest acknowledgment of any weaknesses in your proposal can help build trust with your supervisor.

Now let's consider actions that can help you demonstrate your expertise to your boss:

- **Research your ideas.** Find out everything you can about the idea you are proposing—by talking with knowledgeable individuals, reading relevant sources, and so forth. Collect pertinent data and information to support and contradict your idea so that you are well versed on the idea's strengths and weaknesses.

- **Get firsthand experience.** Participate in cross-functional teams that provide new insights into particular markets, products, or business processes, so you can draw from this knowledge and experience in presenting ideas to your boss.

- **Cite trusted sources.** Support your proposal or position with knowledge gained from trusted sources within or outside your organization. For instance, if you want your boss to support the installation of a new customer database for your department, share testimonials from managers at other, similar organizations that have generated valuable business results by using the database you're recommending.

- **Prove it.** Launch small pilot projects to demonstrate that your ideas deserve serious consideration. For example, if you're advocating a new way of resolving customer problems in your department, conduct a limited experiment with the process to generate firsthand information about its benefits that you can then share with your manager.

Identifying priorities

Frequently, you will need to negotiate with your manager to set or revise your priorities—decisions about what tasks or projects you will accomplish, in what order, and when. If problems arise in your work or you take on new responsibilities, you'll have to renegotiate your priorities and their accompanying due dates immediately with your boss. Don't wait until you are about to miss key deadlines or deliverables to discuss priorities with your supervisor. Do so as soon as you realize that your priorities will need to change.

When you negotiate priorities, you need to balance your understanding of your work and its impact with your manager's understanding of these things. Be sure to do the following:

- Emphasize that you are aware of the importance of *all* the projects for which you are responsible.

- Be clear about the time requirements of the projects you are juggling and what you can and cannot do.

- Ask for help in scheduling deadlines for new work to avoid negative impacts on other projects. Your manager will appreciate it if you prepare a suggested schedule that meets your new needs and if you ask for her feedback on it.

- Provide alternatives if your priorities do not match your manager's expectations.

NEGOTIATION n 1: a process by which the involved parties resolve matters of dispute by holding discussions and coming to a mutual agreement

---

After you have reached agreement on your new priorities, follow up with an e-mail or memo to demonstrate your commitment and "seal the deal."

Negotiating strategically

Specific strategies can help make your negotiations with your manager as effective as possible. For example, be aware of the language you use. Learn to avoid *you*-centered language, and focus on words like *both*, *we*, and *I*. To illustrate, say, "I'm not clear about this point," instead of "You didn't make that clear to me." Or "If we can meet that schedule, it will be a big benefit to both of us," instead of "Your schedule isn't feasible."

Also be clear that you are acting in the best interests of your manager *and* the organization. That means focusing on a "win–win" approach rather than an "I win, you lose" or "you win, I lose" approach. When you emphasize performance results that benefit both you and your manager, you stand a much better chance of negotiating successfully.

In addition, engage your manager in helping you solve problems. Be sure you have thought through the problem and are asking for assistance and offering ideas for possible solutions, not just "dumping" the problem on your manager. Listen carefully to words and their meaning. Ask for clarification if there is something that you do not understand. Finally, avoid becoming defensive if your manager disagrees with you or provides constructive feedback.

Tip: In negotiating with your manager, avoid arguments. Instead, focus on jointly generating options acceptable to both of you.

What You COULD Do.

Remember David's concern about how to disagree with his boss over a deadline she has demanded?

Here's what the mentors suggest:

While David may worry that he might be perceived as negative or that his comments will trigger a defensive reaction, he needs to constructively address his concerns about the schedule. Otherwise, his working relationship with Maria could crumble. He should meet with Maria to let her know that he thinks the schedule is not feasible. The key to the conversation is to disagree in a constructive manner. David should explain to Maria why he thinks the schedule isn't achievable. He should outline the pitfalls and potential risks. He should then ask questions to develop a better understanding of Maria's viewpoint. At the end of the conversation, he should offer alternative solutions, rather than just raising objections. By working with Maria to come to a shared understanding of the situation, David will align his goals with hers, which will, in turn, benefit everyone.

Tips and Tools

Tools for Managing Up

Understanding Your Manager

By answering the following questions, you will be better prepared to communicate effectively with your manager.

Question	Notes
1. What is my manager's communication style? Reader or listener?	
2. Is my manager a detail-oriented person who prefers facts and figures or a big-picture person who prefers just an overview?	
3. Does my manager prefer to delegate tasks and have minimal involvement in day-to-day progress or to have hands-on, day-to-day involvement in my projects?	
4. What are my manager's key strengths?	
5. What are my manager's primary weaknesses?	
6. What are the hot buttons or triggers that prompt quick reactions?	
7. What is my manager's overall mind-set and view of the world (*e.g., optimist or pessimist, team player or loner*)?	
8. What are my manager's important goals and objectives?	

Understanding Yourself

By answering the following questions, you will gain a better understanding of yourself. This helps you communicate more effectively with your manager.

Question	Notes
1. What is my communication style? Reader or listener?	
2. Am I a detail-oriented person who prefers facts and figures or a big-picture person who prefers just an overview?	
3. Do I perform best with a manager who prefers to delegate tasks and has minimal involvement in day-to-day progress, or do I prefer my manager to be more hands-on with day-to-day involvement in my projects?	
4. What are my key strengths and areas of expertise?	
5. What are my primary weaknesses or blind spots?	
6. What are my hot buttons or triggers that prompt quick reactions?	
7. What is my overall mind-set and view of the world (*e.g., optimist or pessimist, team player or loner*)?	
8. What are my important goals and objectives?	
9. How can I align my wants and needs with those of my manager so that we are both satisfied?	

Monitoring the Effectiveness of Your Relationship with Your Manager

Complete this worksheet every few months to monitor the strengths and weaknesses of your relationship with your manager.

Question	Notes
1. Am I aware of my manager's specific and general expectations of me?	
2. Are these expectations fair and realistic?	
3. Is my manager aware of what I expect in return and what resources I might need?	
4. How much does my manager know about what I have been doing for the past few months? If he or she knows little, how can I correct that?	
5. How well do we get along on a daily basis? Are there conflicts or problems that need to be addressed?	
6. Is our relationship built on trust and reliability? Have I been a trustworthy partner? Do I meet commitments? Am I supportive of my manager in talking to others?	
7. Have I been proactive and taken the primary responsibility for managing this relationship?	
8. What is it that I could do differently to more effectively support my manager?	

Negotiating with Your Manager

Use this worksheet to prepare for a negotiation with your manager.

What is the issue, problem, or opportunity prompting the need for negotiation?

What are the risks and benefits for each of the solutions or approaches I am suggesting?

What are my goals for this negotiation?

What do I think my manager's goals are?

How can I try to influence my manager's mind-set? How can I position my solution or suggestions from his or her point of view?

What benefits can I assure my manager will result from my suggestions or proposal?

What are the results I expect from this negotiation?

What are alternative solutions I can present if my initial solutions are not acceptable to my manager?

Test Yourself

This section offers ten multiple-choice questions to help you identify your baseline knowledge of managing up. Answers to the questions are given at the end of the test.

1. Managing up involves learning as much as you can about your manager's strengths, weaknesses, organizational and personal objectives, and personal interests and preferred working style. That sounds like political maneuvering. What's the difference between managing upward and political maneuvering?

   a. No difference. Managing upward is a more correct and positive way to identify the activities involved, especially when your own motives are not totally self-serving.

   b. The objectives are different. Managing upward is a conscious approach to working with your manager toward mutually agreed-upon goals that are in the best interests of you, your manager, and the organization. Political maneuvering rarely has all three best interests in mind.

   c. Managing upward is a process whereby you and your manager collaborate to move both of you up the management ladder, while political maneuvering has only your interests at heart.

2. How can you best gather information about your manager's strengths, weaknesses, objectives, and preferred working style?

   a. Talk with your manager, use your personal observations, ask fellow employees, and ask other managers.

   b. Gather information primarily by listening carefully to your manager; other sources may not be accurate.

   c. For the first six months, talk with your manager and actively observe him or her. After six months, gather information from fellow employees with whom you have developed good relationships.

3. Who should make the first move in establishing a relationship with your manager? You or your manager?

   a. Your manager should assume the primary responsibility for establishing a relationship with you. If he or she does not make the move, allow up to three months, and then assume the responsibility yourself.

   b. You should assume the primary responsibility for shaping your relationship with your manager.

4. If your manager seems unable or unwilling to articulate his or her expectations for you, what might you do?

   a. Send an informal written memo to your manager that outlines your understanding of those expectations, and ask for feedback and agreement.

   b. Wait a few months, and then bring up the subject again.

c. Bypass your manager and instead ask colleagues and other managers for suggestions on strategies that have worked in the past with your manager.

5. Which of the following should you focus on when presenting to your manager a proposed solution to a problem or an approach to an opportunity?

a. The benefits to be gained by implementing this solution or approach.

b. The features of the solution or approach and how it might be implemented.

c. Your role in implementing the proposed solution or approach.

6. Just as you expect your manager to support your goals, you should do what you can to support his or her goals. Which of the following is *not* a good way to use your influence within the organization to make your manager and team look good?

a. Before trying to influence anyone, make a point of understanding his or her mind-set.

b. Increase your sphere of influence in areas that can affect your manager's goals—for example, other departments, customers, and suppliers.

c. Influence the actions of others over whom you have formal authority by offering advice, providing feedback, and sharing your reactions and perspectives.

7. What common error do most people make when providing information to their supervisors?

    a. Providing too much information too often.

    b. Providing too little information too late.

    c. Providing too much information too late.

8. One suggested strategy for communicating effectively with your manager is to determine whether your manager is more of a "listener" or a "reader." What are the implications of each of these?

    a. Listeners want to read about information first and then discuss it. Readers like to hear an overview first and then read the details.

    b. Listeners want to hear information first and read about it later. Readers like to see written reports first and then talk with you about them.

    c. Listeners are comfortable with overview language and prefer not to have to read details before discussing an issue. Readers want to have a written description, even if it is informal, in front of them at all times.

9. Below are statements a manager might say when negotiating a work assignment with his or her supervisor. Which statement would you *avoid* making?

    a. "If you want me to do the analysis at the same time, you'll have to give me three additional days after the survey."

b. "If we need to include the analysis, we'll have to budget three additional days after the survey."

c. "To include the analysis at the same time, I'll need three additional days after the survey."

10. When presenting a problem to your supervisor, you've identified the problem and explained why it's a problem. What should you do next?

a. Pause and ask your manager about possible solutions or approaches.

b. Identify your solution or approach.

c. Ask whether your manager has any questions.

Answers to test questions

1, b. Managing upward is a conscious approach to working with your manager toward mutually agreed-upon goals that are in the best interests of you, your supervisor, and the organization. Political maneuvering, by contrast, involves only your own interests.

2, a. You can gather information about your manager's strengths, weaknesses, objectives, and preferred working style from conversations with your manager, your personal observations, fellow employees, and other managers. Using all these resources will help ensure that the information you gather is as comprehensive and accurate as possible.

3, b. It is to your benefit to assume the primary responsibility for shaping your relationship with your manager. A proactive approach on your part goes a long way toward establishing trust and rapport. It also lets your manager know, right from the start, the value you place on your relationship with him or her.

4, a. By laying out your understanding of his or her expectations and asking for feedback and agreement, you release your manager from the task of articulating expectations. Not all good managers find it easy to begin conversations about expectations. Once the dialogue has begun, outstanding issues can become part of an ongoing, informal conversation. Continue to ask for feedback on a periodic basis.

If you know that your manager responds better to meetings than to written memos, you could set up a series of informal conversations to discuss mutual roles, responsibilities, and measures of success.

5, a. When discussing a potential solution with your manager, focus on the benefits to be gained. The features of the solution, or how it will be implemented, are less important at this stage.

6, c. This is *not* a good way to use your influence, because you need strategies you would use with people over whom you *lack* formal authority.

7, b. Most managers tend to provide their supervisors with too little information too late. By providing timely and comprehensive information to your supervisor about any issues that affect his or her expectations of you, you build trust and teamwork.

8, b. Listeners want to hear information first and read about it later, while readers like to see written reports first and then talk with you about them. To communicate effectively with your manager, you should adapt your approach to your manager's style preference.

9, a. This statement uses "you-centered" language ("You'll have to"), which is not advisable in negotiating with your manager. "I-centered" or "we-centered" language ("I'll/We'll need three additional days after the survey") gets better results.

10, b. In presenting a problem (or an opportunity), it's important to identify your proposed solution or approach. Most managers prefer to hear about your proposed solutions or approaches, not your problems.

To Learn More

Articles

Billington, James. "The Fundamentals of Managing Up." *Harvard Management Update* (September 1997).

Developing a strong relationship with your boss is a key element in becoming an effective manager. The author discusses the importance of understanding your manager's mind-set and your own, defining expectations of both sides, and choosing an appropriate communication style to build a trusting relationship.

Bossidy, Larry. "What Your Leader Expects of You." *Harvard Business Review* (April 2007).

Bossidy advises forging a boss–subordinate compact with your manager, in which each of you works to clarify and fulfill specific expectations of one another. The author lists and describes the expectations most managers have of their subordinates, and those that most subordinates have of their bosses. When each side fulfills his or her part of the boss–subordinate compact, they, their team, and their company all benefit.

Field, Anne. "Truth or Consequences: Dealing with a Conflict-Averse Boss." *Harvard Management Communication Letter* (April 2005).

When a boss can't communicate directly about problems, the performance of employees in his unit suffers. Employees routinely receive less-than-forthcoming performance appraisals and, thus, get little clear guidance on developing their strengths or overcoming their weaknesses. They find it difficult to get the resources they need to complete a project because the boss refuses to stick up for them. And their productivity suffers because they have to spend an inordinate amount of time and effort finding out what the boss really thinks of them. Fortunately, there are strategies you can employ to force needed discussions without making your boss feel he's being backed into a corner, say communication experts.

Gabarro, John J., and John P. Kotter. "Managing Your Boss." *Harvard Business Review* (January 2005).

Gabarro and Kotter affirm the importance of managing up and offer suggestions for developing a productive working relationship by focusing on achieving compatible work styles, clarifying mutual expectations, keeping your boss informed, being dependable and trustworthy, and selectively drawing on your manager's time and resources to meet the most important goals—yours, hers, and the company's.

Harvard Business School Publishing. "Five Questions About Interviewing Your Prospective Supervisor: With Rich Wellins." *Harvard Management Update* (October 2004).

There is nothing more important than an employee's relationship with her boss. But although most hiring managers will look at the personality fit between themselves and the job candidates, few prospective employees give this much consideration—often to their regret if they discover later on that they and their supervisors are mismatched. There are ways for job candidates to hedge against this fate, says Rich Wellins, whose work focuses on helping companies put the right people in the right seats. His advice about how to initiate frank discussions with prospective supervisors—and how to get telltale glimpses into their personalities—is as relevant to considering a new internal assignment as it is to interviewing for a position in a different company.

Harvard Business School Publishing. "How to Speedread People." *Harvard Management Communication Letter* (April 1999).

In their new book, *The Art of Speedreading People*, Paul Tieger and Barbara Barron-Tieger use the Meyers-Briggs Type Indicator as the basis for advice on how you can adjust your communication style to match the personality type of the person with whom you're communicating. This article summarizes the highlights from the book.

Harvard Business School Publishing. "Narcissistic Leaders." *Harvard Management Communication Letter* (June 2000).

Many companies are discovering that "there is no substitute for narcissistic leaders in this age of innovation," as Michael Maccoby writes in a *Harvard Business Review* article, referring to those brash and thoroughly egotistical visionaries that so often head up a company. If Maccoby is right, knowing how to communicate with narcissistic bosses will be nothing short of a strategic management skill in the years ahead. *HMCL* offers some pointers for dealing with the raging narcissist in the corner suite.

Lovett, Paul D. "Meetings That Work: Plans Bosses Can Approve." *Harvard Business Review* OnPoint Enhanced Edition (2000).

The plan meeting is where a project becomes real; it is where people make the decision to go forward with an idea or not. Yet managers often overload a plan presentation with unimportant facts or simply supply inadequate information. CEOs want four questions answered before they'll approve a plan: What is the plan? Why is it recommended? What are the goals? How much will it cost? You should be able to answer each of these questions clearly and in a way that can lead to an agreed-upon course of action.

Books

Boccialetti, Gene. *It Takes Two: Managing Yourself When Working with Bosses and Other Authority Figures.* San Francisco: Jossey-Bass, 1995.

This book tells not how to manage your boss but how to manage yourself in the relationship with your boss. Based on extensive research, the book maps the patterns of people's responses to authority and provides guidance on how to change yourself and the relationship to be more effective.

Chambers, Harry E. *Getting Promoted: Real Strategies for Advancing Your Career*. Reading, MA: Perseus Press, 1999.

Chambers, president of an Atlanta-based consulting and training firm, lays out workplace truths and challenges that can affect upward movement these days, as well as key skills that could boost the possibility of internal promotion.

Coates, Jonathan. *Managing Upwards*. Hampshire, England: Gower Publishing Limited, 1994.

This book presents an overview of the concept of managing upward and provides answers to these questions: Why manage up? What does managing up contribute to an organization? What processes can I use to learn how to manage upward more effectively? The author provides a variety of case examples to illustrate his points and includes specific suggestions for learning how to manage up more effectively.

Smith, Douglas K. *Taking Charge of Change: 10 Principles for Managing People and Performance*. Reading, MA: Addison-Wesley Publishing, 1996.

In this book, the author presents a set of management principles aimed at assisting people in organizational settings to learn new skills and behaviors in response to change. The book is divided into three parts. Part 1 provides an overview of the principles involved in managing performance and change and recommends a focus on performance results and assertive leadership to bring about change. Part 2 moves into a discussion of specific strategies for managing performance and change and diagnostic tools that may be useful in that process. Part 3 focuses on the importance of establishing a vision for the future in leading an organization through a period of change.

eLearning Programs

Influencing and Motivating Others. Boston: Harvard Business School Publishing, 2001.

Have you ever noticed how some people seem to have a natural ability to stir people to action? *Influencing and Motivating Others* provides actionable lessons on getting better results from direct reports (influencing performance), greater cooperation from your peers (lateral leadership), and stronger support from your own boss and senior management (persuasion). Managers will learn the secrets of "lateral leadership" (leading peers), negotiation and persuasion skills, and how to distinguish between effective and ineffective motivation methods. Through interactive cases, expert guidance, and activities for immediate application at work, this program helps managers to assess their ability to effectively persuade others, measure motivation skills, and enhance employee performance.

Leadership Transitions. Boston: Harvard Business School Publishing, 2001.

Whether you are taking on a new position in your current company or starting in a new organization, *Leadership Transitions* will help you succeed. This performance support resource, built with the expertise of Michael Watkins, arms managers with the knowledge they need when they need it. Managers will learn to diagnose situations, assess vulnerabilities, accelerate learning, prioritize to succeed, work with a new boss, build teams, create partnerships, and align units. The program consists of a wide array of assessments and planning tools that learners can use throughout a transition period.

Persuading Others. Harvard ManageMentor. Boston: Harvard Business School Publishing, 2007.

This topic in the renowned Harvard ManageMentor series provides additional information on how to persuade your manager to see the value of your ideas and to take action that will benefit your team and company. You'll learn how to build your credibility with your boss and gauge her receptivity to your ideas. Additional sections explain how to structure a proposal to your boss effectively, provide compelling evidence for how your idea will benefit the department or company, and use vivid language to convince your boss of the merits of your idea.

Sources for Managing Up

The following sources aided in development of this topic:

Alessandra, Tony, and Phil Hunsaker. *Communicating at Work*. New York: Simon & Schuster, 1993.

Bossidy, Larry. "What Your Leader Expects of You." *Harvard Business Review* (April 2007).

Coates, Jonathan. *Managing Upwards*. Hampshire, England: Gower Publishing Limited, 1994.

Dobson, Deborah Singer, and Michael Singer. *Managing Up: 59 Ways to Build a Career-Advancing Relationship with Your Boss*. New York: AMACOM, 2000.

Gabarro, John J., and John P. Kotter. "Managing Your Boss." *Harvard Business Review* (January 2005).

High Performance Management. The Interactive Manager Series. Boston: Harvard Business School Publishing, 1995.

Simpson, Liz. "Why Managing Up Matters." *Harvard Management Update* (August 2002).

Temme, Jim. "Working Effectively with Your Supervisor," in *Productivity Power: 250 Great Ideas for Being More Productive*. Mission, KS: Skillpath Publications, Inc., 1993.

Notes

Notes

Notes

Notes

Notes

Notes

Notes

Notes

Notes

Notes

Notes

How to Order

Harvard Business Press publications are available worldwide from your local bookseller or online retailer.

You can also call:
1-800-668-6780

Our product consultants are available to help you 8:00 a.m.–6:00 p.m., Monday–Friday, Eastern Time. Outside the U.S. and Canada, call: 617-783-7450.

Please call about special discounts for quantities greater than ten.

You can order online at:
www.HBSPress.org